Table of Contents

Note: While reading the book, check out our Youtube channel "Refuge Cities". There you can listen to a playlist that goes along with each chapter. This will add to your experience....at least I hope it does!

Introduction

With the world becoming more unstable everyday, people are getting a little nervous about the future. Many are asking, "can I rely on food sources?" "What can I do about rising prices?" "What will happen if I lose my job?" "What if the world shuts down again?" Chances are, if you picked up this book, you have those same gnawing questions yourself. Questions about sustainability are valid concerns.

One does not have to search hard to find books, television shows, blogs, TikToks, podcasts or Ted Talks about how to survive the Apocalypse. While it is trending right now to be "prepping," I want to advise you on not only how to survive the coming turbulence but to also thrive in what comes AFTER the end of the world as we know it.

This book is not about building the best bunker, and stockpiling just the right stuff- and planning for EVERY possible scenario- an impossible and anxiety-inducing task! This book is not about hunkering down in your Doomsday shelter to wait it out. It is about working together. The ultimate goal of our communities is to make sure no one is left behind. I am writing this in the 1st person because this is my conversation with you. I hope to inspire you to courage. Things in the world ARE intensifying, but now is the time to take bold actions. Join me as I share with you my journey on preparing for the future using ancient wisdom and forgotten knowledge on survival.

What is a City of Refuge?

So that we fully understand the concept of the God-given city of refuge- we must understand the context surrounding such a gift. The first city of refuge was during the time of Moses. The instructions were given to Moses (the leader of Israel at the time) and recorded in the Books of the Law (Numbers and Deuteronomy).

To give some background information, I should mention the Levites. The people of Israel are divided in to 12 tribes, but the land was divided into only 11 portions. The tribe that did not get any land of their own was the tribe of Levi. This tribe was set apart for the purpose of priestly duties. The members of the tribe of Levi worked in the temple/tabernacle offering sacrifices among many other sacred functions. They were interspersed among the other tribes in a community service role, and in turn, it was the duty of the 11 tribes of Israel to care for their community service workers. Part of this arrangement included an allotment of 48 cities with pasture land across the country that would belong to the Levites for their needs. Out of those 48 cities, 6 were designated as cities of refuge.

These strategically placed cities were used for the benefit of anyone accused of murder to be safe until a trial could be held. The priests of these cities were to maintain order and keep blood from needlessly being shed due to revenge. Later in history, it seems that all 48 Levite cities functioned on some level as a sanctuary city. Unintentional homicides were quite curious.

It should be noted, that anyone convected of intentional murder would not be harbored. A guilty verdict of murder would result in capital punishment. The provision of the city of refuge was expressly for those who had committed accidental murder.

The perpetrator of the unintentional killing would reside in the city of refuge until the death of the high priest. At which point, the accused was allowed to return to his/her home town with no penalty. It was understood that the death of the high priest was a substitute for the murder and this death would fulfill the guilt of the manslaughter. This is a beautiful picture of Jesus being the high priest who had given his life so that the rest of us may walk free from any guilt! There would be a payment for the blood of the accidental death not by the perpetrator of the death but by the most innocent of society who would be the high priests of the whole country.

Key Take-aways:
-Land was donated by the 11 tribes to the Levites
-Land was administered and inhabited by the priestly tribe
-All who were accused of murder were welcomed and harbored until a trial was completed
-Life was preserved in these places
-Grace and Mercy were generously applied to those who committed manslaughter
-Hospitality was extended even to accused murderers.

City Building after the End of the World

According to the Biblical account of early history, the earth was destroyed by a worldwide flood. As far as we know, Noah the ark builder, is the only person to have been in the position of rebuilding life as he knew it- after LITERALLY the end of the world. Therefore, I thought it wise to see if there was any record of his opinions on the matter. I was not disappointed.

In the book of Jubilees (a book given to Moses at Mount Sinai), Noah gives his three sons interesting advice passed down from his great grandfather Enoch, on how to establish cities and ultimately a strategy for a successful repopulation of earth.

Book of Jubilees 7:35-38
And behold, ye will go and build for yourselves cities, and plant in them **all** the plants that are upon the earth, and moreover **all fruit-bearing trees**.
For three years the fruit of everything that is eaten will not be gathered: and in the fourth year its fruit will be accounted holy [and they will offer the first-

fruits], acceptable before the Most High God, who created heaven and earth and all things. Let them offer in abundance the first of the wine and oil (as) first-fruits on the altar of the Lord, who receives it, and what is left let the servants of the house of the Lord eat before the altar which receives (it).

And in the fifth year make ye the release so that ye release it in righteousness and uprightness, and ye shall be righteous, and all that you plant shall prosper.

The modern term for what Noah is describing is called permaculture or a food forest. He instructed his children to build cities with every plant/herb that are on the earth and every fruit bearing tree inside the cities. In other words, Noah told them to build urban agricultural city centers. Many great resources are out there on the subject of permaculture- so I'll just say that it's absolutely worth learning more about. I am beyond convinced that permaculture is the most sustainable way to grow food and sustain large populations at scale. What this means is that in a last days desperate situation, we learn from Noah here that you can grow huge amounts of food with a fairly small group of people on relatively small plots of land.

Definition of terms I am using:
-Permaculture = developing an agricultural ecosystem that is to be
sustainable and self-sufficient
-Monoculture = cultivating of a one single crop in a particular area such as a 10 acre plot of land exclusively growing corn
-Food Forest = Mimics a natural growing forest using edible plants.

There are **7 layers** of growth in a food forest instead of 1 in monoculture. Here is a description of those layers:
1. Over-story tree layer (big trees)
2. Under-story tree layer (smaller trees)
3. Shrub layer (berry bushes)
4. Herbaceous layer (mint)
5. Root layer (potatoes)
6. Ground cover layer (flowers, strawberries, garlic)
7. Vine layer (grapes)

Stats on food forest permaculture growing potential:
-**High Productivity** Can produce 15,000-50,000 pounds of food per acre (production rates differ

wildly depending on many variables such as climate, types of plants, and water availability.
-**Resilience** With all the layers of the food forest, you have built in systems that reduce the risk of total crop failure. For example, a late cold snap might kill off the blooms of the apricot tree but also may enhance the growth of the apple tree to be a bumper crop.
-**High resistance** to pests and disease
-**Weed prevention**. Every space is taken up with something that is useful and productive so there is no room for weeds to grow.
-**Less Land** With this type of growing system, land is used more efficiently and in a more sustainable, healthy way. The benefit for humanity is healthier soil, healthier plants, more nutritious food, and bigger yields.

Later on in the story, Noah' prays to God because his descendants are dying of various sicknesses. He prays to God for a solution and in response, he gets a book of herbal remedies. This is even more reason to have a wide variety of plants at our disposal! We can utilize some of these same plants to heal sicknesses! We only stand to benefit from Noah's ancient wisdom, and the more varied our gardens are- the better off, more resilient we'll be! These instructions are very much valid and useful and applicable in today's context.

Key Take-aways:
-Noah had a plan for rebuilding civilization which was to develop permaculture food forest in their cities.
-Herbs and food can be used for medicinal purposes
-Permaculture increases your resilience for growing food
-This ancient wisdom from Noah is still relevant today for being able to grow large amounts of food in a small foot print with few people.

4th Century Monasteries

Historically, monasteries typically operated independently. They attempted to be a self-reliant community. As the church changed, so did monasteries, depending on the community or religious order. Typically, however monasteries could be divided into two extremes. One was a hermetic life in which monks lived in isolation, and the other, collaborative communal monasteries with an outwardly focused approach. These monasteries served the community and sought to meet needs.

The idea of a monastery first came from the Middle East. Egyptian and Syrian Christians practiced a hermetic monastic tradition. Monks would isolate themselves from the world and devote themselves to prayer. Later, a man by the name of Basil of Caesarea (born 330 AD and died 379 AD in modern-day Turkey) would innovate and forever change the idea and purpose of the monastery. Basil traveled through Egypt, Syria, and throughout Western Asia studying monasticism, and for a short time he embraced the lifestyle of solitude. In some ways he liked it, but he felt that time should be dedicated to engagement with the community through labor.

He is considered to be the founder of the Eastern Orthodox Church's ideas on monastic communities and a major influencer and source of inspiration for the establishment of the monastic orders in the Western Church. Basil believed wealth should be used to feed the poor, clothe the destitute, and provide medicine to the sick. He organized the monasteries to be self-sustainable centers where food and wealth generation could thrive. The resources monasteries were able to generate were then reinvested back into the community. He established hospitals inside the monasteries which were open to the public. He built accommodations called poor houses where all homeless were welcomed. He set up a program to give thieves and prostitutes a life away from crime. He personally organized a soup kitchen during a famine. One of his greatest accomplishments was the construction of the Basiliad. This was a very large complex which enabled more of these activities. The land that the Basiliad was constructed on was donated by the regional ruler. Basil believed that communities of Jesus should be dedicated to lavish generosity, sacrificial hospitality with the intention of shining God's light of goodness into the community. He believed that we are supposed to be the hands that God uses to bless the world. He taught that the accumulation and hoarding of wealth is evidence that one does not truly understand the gospel and the example that Jesus was to the world. During Jesus's three year ministry, he spent much of his time healing the sick and feeding multitudes who flocked to hear him teach. He taught his followers to do as he had done which is to care for the forgotten.

Here is one of Basil's most famous quotes:

"The bread you store belongs to the hungry. The clothes you accumulate belong to the naked. The shoes that you have in your closet are for the barefoot. The money you bury deep into the ground to keep it safe, belongs to the poor. You were unfair to as many people as you could have helped and you did not."

Key Takeaways:
-Land was donated by the local ruler
-Land was administered by the priest Basil
-Life was preserved through growth of food and hospitals
-Hospitality was a central principle including thieves and prostitutes

-The goods which were not needed for charity were sold in the market

18th century Spanish Alamo Mission

Basil was an early example of a continuation and innovation of the levite cities of refuge. Now I want to jump forward into history to a more recent iteration brought to North America by the Spanish.

We can all agree that the Spanish did some fairly terrible things in the name of God as they spread their empire around the world. However, was it all bad? Let's look at the Alamo Mission, for an example. The Alamo Mission was founded in 1718 as a missionary outpost between East Texas missions and Mexico. It was called San Antonio de Valero. This mission was in close proximity to a native American tribe called the Coahuiltecans. The missionaries founded the mission with the support of 5 Coahuiltecan men who had become Christians. By 1744, the mission had more than 300 local people, 2,000 cattle, 1,300 sheep, yearly corn production of 2,000 bushels of corn (approximately 100,000 pounds), cotton farm, and a textile workshop for clothing and other cloth related products.

In the early 1800's, colonialization would move into North America, and other Europeans would effectively move the Native Americans out. However, the Spanish took a different approach. They decided to try to Hispanicize them, or make them Spanish. There are obvious glaring problems with this thinking, but in a very flawed way it seemed as if they were trying to coexist with the Native people. Something that was absolutely not an option for the other colonizing powers that came after them would do.

This premise led to the establishment of missions with the purpose to integrate with the locals and teach them Spanish ways. Instead of taking their land, they brought education, workshops and agriculture. They helped provide food and helped the locals to have jobs weaving textiles that they could then sell. The mission in San Antonio served as a sanctuary for the Coahuiltecans when the brutal Comanche would raid and kill everyone. Later in its history, the Alamo was credited for being the first hospital in Texas. The Spanish missions in Texas were a humanitarian effort. The missionaries were trying to preserve life when the politicians and rulers only wanted to control and dominate.

The Alamo is famous today for the battle that took place there during the Texas war for independence from Mexico where Daniel Boon, David Crockett and General Travis died. It did function as a fort to defend against the raids from the Comanche but its primary function and the intention for the establishment of the Alamo was to be a strategy of the Spanish to evangelize the natives and provide a pathway for integration of both societies. The Spanish missionaries went seeking to bless and provide economic opportunity to the locals with sustainability as the primary goal. Ultimately, the Alamo was a third culture. The Spanish Empire wanted to dominate the Americas while the missionaries wanted to spread the gospel. It is hard to spread the good news of Jesus while subjugating and murdering everyone...right? Sadly, the Spanish governors were not always supportive of the missions which led to their slow demise over the ensuing century. The legacy of the Alamo lives on as a successful effort to preserve life and extend radical hospitality.

It is sad that it seems much of the cultural legacy of the local native peoples of Texas was lost. But in truth, not all of the native culture was destroyed- it was adopted. Texas became a melting pot of Native American, Spanish, German and American settlers. Being from Texas, I would argue that the missions in Texas set a unique precedent that we can work together and value each other's culture, and eventually even adopt it. While I do not like that the Spanish implemented cultural appropriation, there was at least one positive result. The culture of Texas today is one of cultural fusion and inclusion practiced even to this day.

Tejano is a uniquely Texan genre of music which has its roots in San Antonio. The word "Tejano" is the word we use for the original local inhabitants of Texas before the Spanish came. My wife's grandfather was a Tejano from El Paso. Their music is a blend of old local ballads using the German accordion playing in a polka style with Spanish lyrics. All three cultures together in one media! If you walk into a Texas restaurant, you'll see a Tex-Mex blend of Spanish and Native American food like BBQ tacos and German beer on the menu all while listening to Tejano music. Not everything was done perfectly, but the enduring legacy of the Texas Missions is one of life preservation rather than repression. Today we celebrate the contributions made by all the groups who have lived in the Lone Star State.

Key Takeaways:
-Mission was strategically placed where there was a need by the regional ruler
-Land was administered by the priest
-The locals were welcomed to live, learn and work
-Life was preserved through growth of food and walls from attackers
-Assimilation was practiced rather than extermination
-Workshops were started for the express purpose of enabling sustainability

Summary

Not everything done in the monasteries or missions of the past would I agree with doing today. We can treat these examples of history like a fish. We can take the meat and leave the bones. Inspiration can be drawn from the cities of refuge which really was the birth of the idea of cities being set apart with people who minister to the community such as the monasteries and missions. These places were outlets for people who have a passion to express their understanding of the sacrificial teachings of Jesus to go to serve. The goal in these havens was to establish sustainable centers of life preservation. The methods they used were to grow food and develop industries which would provide jobs for the poor and generate income which could then be used for expansion of economic opportunity. The culture of these communities was to welcome the least of these and to extend generous hospitality to all who came near. We often struggle with the tension between the sacred and the secular. In these places, there is no conflict or tension at all! Industry and agriculture are there to provide jobs and feed people. Housing and hospitality are available so that those in need are not left destitute

Last Days Principles

There are many interpretations of Daniel and Revelation, and I do not want to go down that rabbit hole, but I hope we can all agree that regardless of how you interpret these passages, what we should be doing is indisputable. We are supposed to be letting our light shine in a dark world. How should we do that? We are to love people. Now that we have that out of the way, let's take a look at what Jesus said to his disciples about the last days and the end of the world in Matthew 24-25. The application of what Jesus said here applies to us today regardless of your beliefs about the last days.

Here is a break down of the passage with more explanation to follow:

24:1-2   Prophecy of Temple destruction
24:3   Disciples ask for the signs of the end of the world
24:4-14   Jesus gives the signs before the end of the world
24:15-26   Jesus gives instructions for what to do after the abomination of desolation
24:27-31   Jesus describes his return
24:32-35   Parable of the fig tree

24:36-44   Parable of the good man not knowing the hour
24:45-51   Parable of the faithful and wise servant
25:1-13   Parable of the 10 virgins
25:14-30   Parable of the 2 stewards
25:31-46   Jesus return and judgement of the Sheep and goats

24:1-2   Prophecy of Temple destruction

In the Spring of 70 A.D, Titus (who was the son of emperor Vespasian) penetrated the last wall protecting Jerusalem. Josephus chronicled that a lone Roman soldier threw a torch at a famous tapestry that was hanging on the wall which Herod commissioned for the temple. They were not able to put out the fire. The massive conflagration burnt the temple completely. After the fire burnt out, the Romans then began to dismantle the entire temple mount just as Jesus had said. Some say the wall that surrounded the temple still remains which we call the wailing wall. At any rate, the Roman destruction of the temple was so complete that there has been debate in modern times as to the true location of the first two temples. Jesus' prophecy was fulfilled around 40 years after he said that it would be destroyed.

24:3   Disciples ask for the signs of the end of the world

The disciples had just proudly showed Jesus the vast and beautiful temple complex and Jesus announced that it will be destroyed utterly. I would imagine that to their mind this would sound like the end of the world. How could they imagine a world without a temple to worship in and make sacrifices for the sins of the people? They would soon understand that Jesus would be the final sacrifice and that our bodies would be the temple for the Spirit to dwell in. There soon would be no longer a need for a physical temple to do sacrifices because Jesus was about to offer his body to be sacrificed as the lamb of God. The hard realization that the temple would be destroyed prompted them to ask about the signs for the end of the world and Jesus' return.

24:4-14   Jesus gives the signs before the end of the world

The signs are:

Stage 1: Beginning of Sorrows 24:4-8
    -Many false messiahs 24:5
    -Wars and rumors of wars 24:6
    -Famine 24:7

-Earthquakes 24:7
-Epidemics 24:7

Stage 2: Severe Persecution 24:9-13
-Will be delivered for persecution 24:9
-Will be killed 24:9
-Saints will be hated by all nations because of Jesus name 24:9
-Betrayal of one another 24:24:10
-Hate each other 24:10
-Many false prophets will rise and deceive 24:11
-Love will turn cold 24:12

Promise: He who endures to the end will be saved! 24:13
-In the middle of all of these signs of the times, Jesus gives us a promise. He says that those who endure to the end will be saved!

Stage 3: Jesus Gospel will be Preached to all the Nations 24:14

Stage 4: The Beginning of the End: (starts with the abomination of desolation 24:15-26)

Jesus gives instructions on what to do after the abomination of desolation:

-Those in Judea are to flee to the mountains 24:16 (perhaps to Petra?)
-Do not take anything....just run! 24:17-18
-Pray that the flight will not be in Winter or on the Sabbath 24:20
-Do not listen to rumors of Jesus' return. Do not go out and seek out the false messiahs 24:23-26

27-31 Jesus describes his return

-Jesus will come on a cloud from the Eastern sky 24:27, 24:30
-After the tribulation of those days, the Sun and moon will be darkened 24:29
-Stars will fall (perhaps demons) 24:29
-Powers of the heavens will be shaken 24:29
-All will see Jesus on the clouds 24:30
-Angels will sound a trumpet and gather the elect 24:30

24:32-35 Parable of the fig tree

32 Now learn a parable of the fig tree; When his branch is yet tender, and putteth forth leaves, ye know that summer is nigh:
33 So likewise ye, when ye shall see all these things, know that it is near, even at the doors.

Here, we have a continuation of Jesus's teachings on the fig tree. Jesus is using the blooming of the fig tree as a sign of the end of the world and his return. Jesus had been talking about the fig tree that had not been fruitful in many places in the gospels.

People interpret this passage in different ways, even among friends, we disagree on the meaning of what Jesus was talking about! I will share with you my understanding of the meaning based on the belief that we should interpret scripture with scripture.

On the same occasion (mentioned in other gospels), Jesus likens Israel to a fig tree which he then curses because it does not produce fruit. Also, in many Old Testament references, Israel is represented as a fig or fig tree.

Who is the generation that will not have passed away until all these things should be fulfilled? It makes it very doubtful that the generation would be referring to the first century church. It seems that Jesus curses Israel or Jerusalem because of unfruitfulness. The Jews would continue to be subjugated by the Romans and the destruction and devolution of their religious system was imminent. The context of these passages is a question about what are the signs of the end of the world. The world has not ended yet....has it?

My thought is that the signs of the end of days is that Israel will either start producing spiritual fruit or perhaps 1948 was the start as this was the year the nation of Israel was organized in Palestine. In Luke 21:29, this same parable is spoken of. Only in this passage, it mentions the fig tree "AND all the other trees". This is particularly interesting when you consider around the same time Israel was founded at the end of World War 1, the Ottoman empire ended in 1922. The British and the French helped the neighbors of Israel get started. We could say the Date Tree or the Phoenix Palm was The unification of Saudi Arabia under Abdul Aziz Al Saud in 1932 or perhaps in 1945 when Saudi Arabia was admitted into the United Nations. Then in 1946, we had the independent Hashemite Kingdom of Transjordan which would be the Oak Tree. The famous Cedar Tree would be established in Lebanon with the independence from the French declared on 22nd of November

1943. On October 24, 1945, Syria gained their independence. They were also a founding member of the United Nations that year. The national tree of Syria is the Olive Tree. In my estimation, this passage seems to be playing out in our lifetime. According to Mark 11, Jesus goes up to Jerusalem to cleanse the temple with a whip and just before he gets to the temple, he comes to a fig tree that has no fruit buds. This was not the time of harvest for the figs as that is in the Summer. This was the time where the fruit buds would form in early Spring. Jesus saw that there was no potential for fruit on the tree. It only had leaves. According to the Luke account of this time frame of leading up to the crucifixion week, he mentions that Jesus gave a parable about a fig tree that did not produce fruit. The garden keeper pleaded with the master to allow him to fertilize and give the tree another chance to bear fruit before pulling it up. Jesus gives the application of that parable just before he gave this parable about the end of the world by saying that anyone who does not repent will perish. Towards the end of this passage he then laments over Jerusalem. The evidence is fairly overwhelming.

It appears that after giving all these lessons about the fig tree and in connection with a demand for repentance, Jesus goes up to the temple to challenge and cleanse it from the vipers who were occupying it. The temple of God in Jerusalem had several sections. The holy of holies was restricted to the high priest who would make atonement of sin for all the people once per year. The inner court is where Jews were allowed to meet with the priests and offer sacrifices for sins as they would repent of discovered sin. The outer court was reserved for the gentiles to come for prayer and worship. The Gentiles were not allowed into the temple any further. The outer area of the Gentiles was the largest portion of the temple complex. This is where the money changers and livestock venders conducted business. According to historians, this area of the gentiles was so full of venders, there was no room for foreign worshipers to even come in. Hundreds of thousands of sheep would be sold in this area over that weekend. It was a huge hustle. Part of the reason I think Jesus was so angry was because the Jew had made the temple mount into a religious casino. They were supposed to welcome the gentiles to come and worship. This area was filled to capacity with the religious mafioso's who were more interested in enriching themselves rather than facilitating reconciliation between the lost of the earth and God. There was no hospitality to the foreigners. There seems to be a clear connection between the discussions Jesus had about the fig tree and his frustration towards unrepentant Jews in Jerusalem.

24:36-44 Parable of the good man not knowing the hour

36 But of that day and hour knoweth no man, no, not the angels of heaven, but my Father only.
37 But as the days of Noah were, so shall also the coming of the Son of man be.
38 For as in the days that were before the flood they were eating and drinking, marrying and giving in marriage, until the day that Noe entered into the ark,
39 And knew not until the flood came, and took them all away; so shall also the coming of the Son of man be.
40 Then shall two be in the field; the one shall be taken, and the other left.
41 Two women shall be grinding at the mill; the one shall be taken, and the other left.
42 Watch therefore: for ye know not what hour your Lord doth come.
43 But know this, that if the goodman of the house had known in what watch the thief would come, he would have watched, and would not have suffered his house to be broken up.

No one knows the day or the hour of Jesus' return. Date setting for Jesus' return is folly. It says here in this passage that He will come when no one expects. The advice He gives is clear: we are to watch and to continue being wise and faithful stewards of what He has given us to do. As you will see, He explains it further in the next parable. We cannot know the day or hour, but that does not mean we cannot know the season of His return. As we read the signs of the times, we are wise to know the seasons.

24:45-51 Parable of the faithful and wise servant

49 And shall begin to smite his fellow servants, and to eat and drink with the drunken;
50 The lord of that servant shall come in a day when he looketh not for him, and in an hour that he is not aware of,
51 And shall cut him asunder, and appoint him his portion with the hypocrites: there shall be weeping and gnashing of teeth.

Here he starts off with a riddle. He says, "who then is a faithful and wise servant, whom his lord hath made ruler over his household, to give them meat in due season?". Jesus does not give us the answer. Think about it. Who in scripture was a faithful and wise servant and then became the ruler's right hand man and provided food when there was a great need? I think it was Joseph. It says that the one who is behaving like this faithful servant will be blessed upon Jesus' return. Conversely, the evil servant who says in his heart, "my lord delays his coming" and then begins to attack his fellow servants and to eat and drink with the drunken will be cut apart and appoint his portion with the hypocrites. You may be asking yourself why I am going through Matthew 24 in a book about cities of refuge. This passage is full of advice and warnings that in my opinion point to what we are supposed to be doing as we anticipate the end of the world and Jesus's promise to return at that time on a cloud. Joseph saw what was coming on the horizon. He knew he had to make plans and arrangements so that when hard times came, he would be able to not only rescue his family from starvation but all the nations surrounding Egypt. Egypt was the country of refuge during this great crisis. Unfortunately, the Egyptians used this occasion to enslave all their neighbors and subjugate their land and bodies in exchange for food. I believe we are to be like Joseph but instead of preying on people we are to pray for them. We are not to abuse the destitute of the last days but like our example in Basil, we are to lift them up and empower them through love-filled holy hospitality. Here, we have a promise. Those who are found to be like Joseph upon Jesus return, will be blessed! So the natural questions begs asking, " How can we be like Joseph?"

Joseph provided a haven for his siblings and father when they became refugees. Even though his brothers sold him into slavery, he ensured their safety. God may give you an opportunity to bless those who have hurt you. If we are to be like Joseph, we have to be prepared physically to meet peoples needs and spiritually to have a heart of compassion to serve those who least deserve it. We must be prepared in the heart and mind to forgive those who may have even hated you!

I believe that the leaders of cities of refuge should have the ethos of Joseph. They should be good stewards and be servants to all. They need to be forgiving and yet strong leaders who are unwavering in the face of severe persecution.

25:1-13 Parable of the 10 virgins

1 Then shall the kingdom of heaven be likened unto ten virgins, which took their lamps, and went forth to meet the bridegroom.
2 And five of them were wise, and five were foolish.
3 They that were foolish took their lamps, and took no oil with them:
4 But the wise took oil in their vessels with their lamps.
5 While the bridegroom tarried, they all slumbered and slept.
6 And at midnight there was a cry made, Behold, the bridegroom cometh; go ye out to meet him.
7 Then all those virgins arose, and trimmed their lamps.
8 And the foolish said unto the wise, Give us of your oil; for our lamps are gone out.

9 But the wise answered, saying, Not so; lest there be not enough for us and you: but go ye rather to them that sell, and buy for yourselves.
10 And while they went to buy, the bridegroom came; and they that were ready went in with him to the marriage: and the door was shut.
11 Afterward came also the other virgins, saying, Lord, Lord, open to us.
12 But he answered and said, Verily I say unto you, I know you not.
13 Watch therefore, for ye know neither the day nor the hour wherein the Son of man cometh.

This is perhaps the second scariest warning and parable in this passage. Who do you think the virgins represent? Some say, the church is referenced as the bride of Christ in 2 Corinthians 11:2 and you might make a case for Ephesians 5:21-24, but Jerusalem and the new Jerusalem are also referenced as the bride of Christ in Revelation 21. Needless to say, disagreements abound over who or what is the bride of Christ. Some would say it is the redeemed of the Church while others would say it is the New Jerusalem. If we look at this parable in the context of the other parables in this passage, what is the theme? To whom is Jesus warning to be prepared? I am not going to answer this directly now. Let us continue to go through this passage and see what becomes clear.

Who are the ten virgins exactly and what do they represent?

In the parable, ten virgins are waiting for the return of their bridegroom. Five virgins are prepared with oil, and five took no oil with them. While the bridegroom was gone, ALL slept. At midnight, a cry was made that the bridegroom was on the way. The foolish virgins realized they would not be able to go out and meet the bridegroom at night because they had no oil. So, they asked the wise for oil but there was not enough to go around. These foolish brides ran out to try and quickly buy oil so they could be taken by the bridegroom....but to no avail. He came and took those who were already burning oil. Can you see why I find this passage terrifying? With all of prophetic scriptures coming to fulfillment in our days, has the midnight cryer already notified us of the return of the bridegroom? Is there time for the foolish to get oil?

Why would you need oil in your lamp? To burn is the answer. The wise were ready to shine their light at a moment's notice. Just like Basil from Turkey, he had already grown the food at his monastery before the famine broke out. He was wise and prepared to launch his food kitchen to make sure no lives were lost due to starvation. Oil is often a symbol of the Holy Spirit in Scripture. We need the help of the Spirit of God to show us how to prepare for His return. However, in order to be ready to shine then- we must be prepared and shining NOW! We are not called to be hiding in a bunker full of food waiting for Jesus to return. Jesus is coming back for a bride who is shining brightly in the midst of persecution and famine to serve and rescue the least of these. It appears that Jesus will leave the fools behind. It will take faith and courage to shine in these last days. The more violent and harsh the world treats the lovers of Jesus, the harder it will be to shine, but the alternative is to be a fool and be left behind.

The reason I think they are called fools is because they were not prepared to serve and bless the destitute both spiritually and physically. This will become clear more when we get to the Sheep and goat judgement in a moment. I believe we who believe in Jesus should be preparing not just to ride out the apocalypse in a comfy hole in the ground but we are to serve our communities and make sure there are none left out in the cold who are hungry and naked. This will be our time as the bride of Christ to step up and make him proud! To preserve life and to be prepared to shine during the darkest period of human history. It will be easy for the bridegroom to find his bride because she is already shinning. The wise brides will not be stumbling through the darkness because they have adequate oil. They will easily be spotted and found because they have been shining with plenty of oil.

I do think it is possible that the 10 virgins represent Jerusalem on some level. Perhaps the 5 virgins who have oil represent the "first fruits" mentioned in Revelation 14:1-5. Regardless of who precisely this parable is referring to, the application for us is clear. We want to be wise with oil in our torch. We should be ready with anticipation to the return of Jesus and burning brightly so that we can walk through the night.

25:14-30 Parable of the 2 stewards

14 For the kingdom of heaven is as a man travelling into a far country, who called his own servants, and delivered unto them his goods.
15 And unto one he gave five talents, to another two, and to another one; to every man according to his several ability; and straightway took his journey.
16 Then he that had received the five talents went and traded with the same, and made them other five talents.
17 And likewise he that had received two, he also gained other two.

18 But he that had received one went and digged in the earth, and hid his lord's money.
19 After a long time the lord of those servants cometh, and reckoneth with them.
20 And so he that had received five talents came and brought other five talents, saying, Lord, thou deliveredst unto me five talents: behold, I have gained beside them five talents more.
21 His lord said unto him, Well done, thou good and faithful servant: thou hast been faithful over a few things, I will make thee ruler over many things: enter thou into the joy of thy lord.
22 He also that had received two talents came and said, Lord, thou deliveredst unto me two talents: behold, I have gained two other talents beside them.
23 His lord said unto him, Well done, good and faithful servant; thou hast been faithful over a few things, I will make thee ruler over many things: enter thou into the joy of thy lord.
24 Then he which had received the one talent came and said, Lord, I knew thee that thou art an hard man, reaping where thou hast not sown, and gathering where thou hast not strawed:
25 And I was afraid, and went and hid thy talent in the earth: lo, there thou hast that is thine.
26 His lord answered and said unto him, Thou wicked and slothful servant, thou knewest that I

To recap, we have had two parables with two
groups in each parable: a wise servant/bride and a
foolish servant/bride. Here we will continue that
trend. Only this time, there will be two types of
stewards. This parable starts off with a man who is
traveling to a far off country. Before he leaves, he
will deliver his goods to his servants to invest on
his behalf while he is away. Two servants
managed to double their holdings, but one servant
buried his portion. When the lord returned, he
commended the faithful stewards who doubled
their holdings and rewards them by making them
rulers of many things. However, the lord was
angry with the steward who only buried his
holdings. He repossessed his holdings, and threw

him into outer darkness where there was weeping and gnashing of teeth. It sounds like hell to me.

This parable seems like an extension of all the other parables in this passage only this time, the reason for not being faithful was fear.

This parable is building to the climax of the passage; Jesus seems to explain the other parables by giving this one.The steward who buried his investment, was afraid. He hid what he had because he did not want to lose it, but the lord was angry when he realized that this steward was only looking out for himself. He was not willing to take any risk for his lord. He was not even willing to put the investment into the bank where it could draw interest. His fear crippled him.

On the flip sides, the lord was proud and happy with the wise stewards who managed to multiply what they had. They took risks to make more and were not afraid to try. What has the Lord given to you? How are you being a good steward?

To me, this is a warning to those who are fearful of persecution. Jesus is saying that the steward who was afraid hid his money out of fear. When the end of days approaches, Jesus makes it clear that Christians will not be popular. We will be hunted and persecuted. I believe Jesus here is saying that we are to be brave and shine brightly even if it cost us everything.

25:31-46 Jesus return and judgement of the Sheep and goats

34 Then shall the King say unto them on his right hand, Come, ye blessed of my Father, inherit the kingdom prepared for you from the foundation of the world:
35 For I was an hungered, and ye gave me meat: I was thirsty, and ye gave me drink: I was a stranger, and ye took me in:
36 Naked, and ye clothed me: I was sick, and ye visited me: I was in prison, and ye came unto me.
37 Then shall the righteous answer him, saying, Lord, when saw we thee an hungred, and fed thee? or thirsty, and gave thee drink?
38 When saw we thee a stranger, and took thee in? or naked, and clothed thee?
39 Or when saw we thee sick, or in prison, and came unto thee?
40 And the King shall answer and say unto them, Verily I say unto you, Inasmuch as ye have done it unto one of the least of these my brethren, ye have done it unto me.

41 Then shall he say also unto them on the left hand, Depart from me, ye cursed, into everlasting fire, prepared for the devil and his angels:
42 For I was an hungred, and ye gave me no meat: I was thirsty, and ye gave me no drink:
43 I was a stranger, and ye took me not in: naked, and ye clothed me not: sick, and in prison, and ye visited me not.
44 Then shall they also answer him, saying, Lord, when saw we thee an hungred, or athirst, or a stranger, or naked, or sick, or in prison, and did not minister unto thee?
45 Then shall he answer them, saying, Verily I say unto you, Inasmuch as ye did it not to one of the least of these, ye did it not to me.
46 And these shall go away into everlasting punishment: but the righteous into life eternal.

With each successive parable, the picture becomes more clear what Jesus wants from us in the last of days before he returns. He does not mince words here in the final statement about his expectations for his people. Again, there are two groups. You have the goats and the sheep. Jesus says that when He returns, He will separate the goats from the sheep. Jesus says specifically that He will gather up and separate all ETHNE. This is where we get the word ethnicity. In

HELPS Word-studies, this word appears as 1484 and says, "(from etho, forming a custom, culture) - people joined by practicing similar customs or common culture; nation(s), usually referring to unbelieving Gentiles (non-Jews)." Jesus says that he is going to separate all the people into culturally distinctive groups.

This makes me think of the judgement of Sodom and Gomorrah. Everyone who was in those cities were judged together. The first thing that pops into my head is...there are Christians in almost every country on Earth. How would that be fair or right? We would all be doomed. There would be no sheep. In my studies, when I came across HELPS Word-studies, it helped me to think of this in terms of people who are joined by similar customs and culture. The Ethos or culture at Amazon is vastly different from Apple. I personally believe that based on the previous parables that Jesus has been sharing that the context of this parable is of those who claim to follow Jesus. The parables of the servants, brides and stewards seem to be pointing to the Lord's people, the people who identify as Christ followers. So in that context, this passage is saying that Jesus is going to separate all the groups that claim to belong to Him into two groups. There will be many church cultures on the right side or in the sheep corner and many church groups in the left side or the goat corner. So how does Jesus determine which group goes where? He tells us.

-There are only two groups here just as in the other parables. Let us examine and separate the two groups characteristics.

Group 1 Characteristics:
      -At the right side of Jesus
      -Called sheep
      -Called wise brides
      -Called faithful servant
      -Were Blessed
      -Courageously invested holdings
      -Like Joseph
      -Had oil
      -Was ready to shine and did shine
      -Was watching, waiting and ready
      -Was taken with the bridegroom
      -Was rewarded
      -Fed the hungry
      -Gave water to the thirsty
      -Showed hospitality to the stranger
      -Clothed the Naked
      -Visited the sick
      -Visited the imprisoned
      -Served the least of these

    -Loved people as though they were Jesus himself
        -Inherited the Kingdom
        -Get eternal Life
        -Givers

Group 2 Characteristics:
        -At the left side of Jesus
        -Called goats
        -Called foolish brides
        -Called evil servant
        -Called wicked slothful servant
        -Fearfully buried holdings
        -Were cursed
        -Not like Joseph
        -Did NOT have oil
        -Was NOT ready to shine and did not shine
        -Was NOT watching, waiting or ready
        -Was left by the bridegroom
        -Was punished
        -Fed NOT the hungry
        -Gave NO water to the thirsty
        -Showed NO hospitality to the stranger
        -Clothed the Naked NOT
        -Visited NOT the sick
        -Visited NOT the imprisoned
        -NEVER served the least of these
        -Loved only themselves

-Sent to the place of everlasting fire with the devil and his angels
   -Get everlasting punishment
   -Takers

I want to share a personal story. It is embarrassing to confess. When I was about 17 years old, I worked for a grocery store in South Texas called HEB. One night, my shift had finished and I was walking out the front door of the store about to go to my car. At the very entrance to the door, a man walked up to me and asked for a penny. He said he only needed one more penny to buy a banana. I reached into my pocket and grabbed a handful of change. With the fist full of coins, I looked him in the eye and said, "I do not have anything to give". He walked into the store and I continued another 15 steps or so. All of the sudden shame came over me. I had just denied a man $.01 cent. I stopped and reached back into my pocket clutching the handful of change with a deep sense of regret. I turned around and ran back into the store to find this man and give him all the coins I had. I knew he had to be in the store because he just walked in behind me. I looked everywhere but he was nowhere to be found! It was almost as if he had vanished into the air. I even frantically checked the restrooms to no avail.

I walked back to my car fully dejected. I could not believe what I had just done. I reckoned that I had failed a test. This must have been an angel or maybe even Jesus himself! "Lord, please forgive me!", I prayed. That moment changed my life. I acted like a goat! Who denies someone a penny! Only a goat would be so selfish. I decided in my heart that I would never be that way again. If I have money to give when someone asks, I always try to give it. Perhaps as I share this story, you might think of goat moments in your life? This does not and should not be the last chapter. We can repent of our goatish ways and live sacrificial sheep lives.

I want to be very clear about something that might be churning in your mind and heart that has in mine. A condemning heart is disheartening. When I think about my failures where God's love could have flowed and I closed my heart to the needs, I have holy grief. Regret can set in and Satan can cause you to question even your salvation. Perhaps there is no conflict in your heart. Maybe you have known you are guilty and need repentance. If you know you are a goat, I have some very good news for you. Next, I will tell you how you can become a sheep.

Doing good works does not save you or make you a sheep. In John 10:7-10, the door of the sheep gate is through a person. His name is Jesus. If you want to be a sheep, it has to be through Jesus. Ephesians 2:8-9 says it is by grace through faith that you can be saved. It is by our repentance or turning away from our failures and sin and turn to Jesus. He then clothes us with his righteousness. Another way to say it is this, we must put our trust in Jesus life to live perfect and without blame. We cannot be perfect but he already did it. Ee shed his blood on the cross. His blood was sprinkled on the mercy seat in heaven on our behalf. It is by faith, that we trust in his blood sacrifice to pacify God's anger and wrath that was directed at us. Moses told the people to put the blood of a lamb on the door post and lentels. This was the first passover which took place directly before the people Israel left the land of Egypt. Every home which had the blood of the lamb over the door post and lentels, was spared from the curse when the angel of death came by that night. Jesus told us that he is the lamb of God who takes away the sins of the world. If you are trusting in your good works to be good enough on judgement day, you will be determined and judged a goat.

Conversely, you can be saying all the right theological things. You can know the Bible inside and out and look right on the outside and also be in danger of eternal damnation. Pharisees were the religious people who thought they knew everything about God and yet they fought with Jesus constantly. Pharisees are experts at missing the point on everything that matters. They strain at a gnat and swallow a camel whole! Pharisees will read a book like this and look for every reason to be critical and look for flaws. The reason is because they need to make themselves feel good about their lack of good works. James 2:14-26 discusses this topic. It says that faith without works is dead and it goes on to say that true faith in Christ always produces good works. This paragraph is written as a warning to modern Pharisees. This is a call to repentance to those who have "good theology" but are selfish. I can speak on this subject with authority because I was a Pharisee. When in college, I came to understand that I was a disgusting person because I thought I was good. My pride was through the roof because of self righteousness. I heard a message on the radio about the people that Jesus was constantly battling. It was the religious people. I immediately felt conviction in my heart. The preacher said, "you are worshiping God and he does not care. You are praying and he will not listen. You fast and he does not care because you are teaching man's doctrines of religion and high as God's law." The preacher then goes on to talk about Isaiah 58. His message was targeting people like me who were outwardly doing all the "good stuff". God is not only disgusted with me but angry. I was at war with God thinking God was lucky to have me on his team. The preacher said, "the fast I would have for you is to clothe the naked, to feed the hungry, to free the slave and to bring relief to those who are oppressed." Immediately I remembered the man at the HEB grocery store who asked me for a penny for a banana. I knew God was angry with me. I broke down in desperate holy repentance. I can love much because I can view my sin of pride and self righteousness as VERY BIG. I was maybe worse than the woman at the well. I was filthier than the woman caught in adultery not because one sin is necessarily worse than another but because my sin had not been dealt with and repented of. I was not a generous person. I was a self-interested person. I cared more about what people thought of me rather than what God thought. I was in a pursuit of more religiosity. I thought spirituality was knowing more about God. What I needed was to know God. Look through this paragraph. How many times did I use the word I? That is all you need to know about what was wrong with me. Works will not save you but faith without works is dead. Doing the outward religious things that are right without love and generosity indicates something is desperately wrong. Bottom line: Pharisees are goats.

Do the last two paragraphs seem like they are contradictory? Works do not make you a sheep. Lack of works indicate you are a goat. There is tension here. This tension is supposed to bring us to a place of introspection. Any good work that is not done in and with love empowered by God, is vain. It is probably selfish on some level. We cannot do what we need to do in our own strength. It has to come from a pure source. Goats are not able to love. Sheep are able to love because they know the gate keeper. You can only become a sheep by faith and repentance.

How do you enter the sheep fold by faith?

This is very simple. So simple in fact, you might miss it. Jesus made it so simple that even a child can do it. Jesus said that he is the only way to God. He also said that there is no way for our sins to be erased and atone for other than through him. In the days and years before Jesus crucifixion and sacrifice, the Jews would offer animal sacrifices to pay for their sins of the pervious year. They had to make these sacrifices every year.

Jesus said that he is the lamb of God who takes away the sins of the world. He laid his life down as a sacrifice and shed his perfect blood on the mercy seat of heaven. What does that mean? It means that when we put our trust in his blood to cover our sins, he says that he will be faithful and just to cleanse us from all unrighteousness. In other words, when we put our faith in Jesus' sacrifice before God, God does not see your sins any longer. It is as though your guilt has been erased. There are no good works that we can do to earn enough points with God to over come our evil deeds. It is not possible. Moses told the people of Israel while they were still in Egypt to put the blood of a lamb on their doors posts and lentels. The reason for this was because an angel was coming to kill all of the first born children of Egypt as a punishment. Anyone who had the blood of the lamb over their home and door would be spared of the consequences of this punishment. You must be covered by the blood of Jesus by faith in his redemptive sacrifice on the cross. The blood needs to be applied to the door of your heart.

If you have not already, I would like to invite you to trust in Jesus blood and ask him to forgive you and apply his blood to your account that you may be blameless before God. Ask Jesus if he would apply his blood to the door of your heart.

How do you repent?

In order to walk through the door of the sheep fold that is stained with Jesus blood, you must repent of your sins. To repent means that you turn away from sinful behavior. You recognize the bad things in your life and you seek to drop them and as best you can run towards good deeds and good works. You must run away from evil deeds. This does not mean you will be perfect. We all fall short of perfection but that does not mean you cannot strive towards godliness. Would you consider turning away from the ways of the world. Would you repent of your sins as you ask God to forgive you and shine as hard and as bright as you can with his Spirit as your fuel?

Becoming a sheep will ensure that you do survive the most dangerous portion of the end of this age. When Jesus returns, the opportunity for repentance will be over. Be prepared in the most important way.

It Started with a Garden and Ends with a Garden

God created a garden for Adam and Eve to live in. Food was abundant and God walked regularly with mankind. Because of the partaking of the forbidden fruit, Adam had to work for and plant his own garden and he lost access to God in the garden.

In the millennial temple described in end of Ezekiel, we see a new garden planted along a river that comes out of the temple and flows out toward the dead sea. Only our Prince is allowed to use the Eastern gate of the temple complex. He regularly walks through that gate and meets with men and women in this new garden!

Features of the Ezekiel Millennial Temple
    -4.48 miles around the perimeter of the outer wall 42:16-20
    -4 kitchens in the 4 corners of the complex 46:21-24
    -Singers and worship area 40:44
    -30 buildings around the inside perimeter of the wall (Dinning Halls?) 40:17-19
    -6 Priestly dining halls. 3 to the North and 3 to the South 42:1-14
    -Fruit trees planted along a river 47:7-12
    -A river flowing from the threshold of the Temple 47:1-6
    -A Sanctuary 41:1-26

-Return of God's Glory 43:1-9
-Eastern Gate Used only by the Prince 44:1-3

This temple seems to be a welcome center
for the nations to come and eat food grown
around the temple, drink the life giving water
flowing from the Sanctuary and have fellowship
with the Messiah or the Prince in the court of the
Temple. In many ways, this temple is a recreation
of the garden of Eden. It restores fellowship
between man and God while providing life giving
food and water. It is more than just a worship
center.

The reason this chapter is included in this
book is to highlight God's plan for fellowship with
mankind. He originally had a fruitful garden which
could sustain the physical needs of Adam and Eve.
He walked among them and had personal
relationships with them. When our Prince returns,
we see that he will utilize a similar template. The
temple will be a place of constant worship, eating
and fellowshipping with him. We may not have
witnessed Jesus return yet but we can create cities
of worship where we imitate this model of
generosity and hospitality. Perhaps this magnifies
the reason Jesus was so angry when he went to
the temple. It was a den of thieves. It was not a
welcome center but a religious casino. Let us live

in the culture of heaven and operate in the same ethos and mindset of the coming millennial temple.

So What Should We Do?

My solution to the Earth's problems? You guessed it! We should build cities of refuge. These sanctuaries will become hubs of light and provision. The sheep will gather in these paddocks of praise and use these monasteries as launching pads for all manner of outreach-oriented endeavors that will meet the needs in each individual community and spread the gospel into the least-reached places of earth. It will break down reaching the least reached peoples into smaller bites. Cities of refuge will be glorious ecosystems where saints with a burden to love courageously will network.

Each refuge will act as a regional hub and they will be connected by bridges of light connecting the whole earth. Champions of generosity and hospitality will be able to easily and quickly jump between the cities to meet the needs where ever they may be.

I believe that we should follow the example of the past and each city of refuge should be administered by the most mature and "Joseph like" leaders. The priests were the administrators of the cities of refuge in the Old Testament; as well as, during the times of the monasteries. The Missionaries oversaw the operations of the Missions. I believe leaders should be raised up in existing cities of refuge where they can be trained and allowed to lead internally before launching them into new locations. Each location should be as autonomous and self sustainable as possible.

A network of cities of refuge enables for these kingdom nodes to be connecting points where bridges of light allow people to easily move freely throughout the earth closing the gaps between opportunities and realization of potential. It makes moving around easier. It makes connecting people with certain skills and the opportunities expeditious. To move a family across a state or country is hard enough, but to move them across the world increases the difficulty level many times over. Because extravagant hospitality should be baked into the culture of cities of refuge, people can feel excited to transition from city to city as needs and opportunities present themselves. These hubs of peace and rest serve as infrastructure to actively meet the needs of the community surrounding it.

You may be sitting there thinking to yourself...I am a sheep but how do I get involved? How do I fit? My answer is simple.

Consider your talents, consider your excesses, consider the needs around you? Ask God for leading. After you asked him, what came to mind? You can give time to volunteer, money to invest or land to donate. If you have no excess to give, then you could come and live with us or another group doing similar things near you. We will find a way for you to be involved. Then you will have excess food to give at an absolute minimum. Living in a city of refuge will give you a front row seat to be the hands of kindness that God wants to use to bless the people of the earth. Everyone has a role to play. No one is more important. The body needs every member to be functional and healthy. You have something to bring to the body that is desperately needed. Come and visit. Our goal is to make it free to stay and eat when you come and visit. You are our guest! If there is not a refuge near you, then lets change that. You can sign up on a list to be apart of a modern monastery. When land is donated in you area, we can have an immediate list of people ready to activate the new location. You can start your own! I would love to see thousands of these places pop up all over the world spontaneously!

We Have Always Needed Cities of Refuge

We now know what a city of refuge is historically, and we explored Matthew 24-25 in terms of the kind of people Jesus is looking for us to be, and we've looked at past examples of sheep like Basil of Caesarea, and considering how we might also be a person with sheep-like qualities. I would like to share a story of a time that we needed a city of refuge; as well as, a story about how I came to the realization that we need refuges for those who will not take the mark of the beast to run to. For those of you who are not familiar with the term "mark of the beast", the book of Revelation in the Bible tells us that there will come a mark that everyone must get either in their forehead or wrist in order to buy or sell. John tells us that everyone who takes the mark will be damned to hell. It appears there will be a need for those of us who will refuse this mark, to have a safe place to run to.

Here is a story about an Arab Christian who was my wife's friend and the unbelievable story that transpired. We will call her Norah. Her journey towards Jesus began when her mother was sick in the hospital. While spending time at the hospital, she encountered a Filipino nurse who loved Jesus. Norah asked the Filipino nurse if she would pray for her mother. She gladly did so. Norah felt so loved by the kindness and care of the nurse that she had to ask if she was a Muslim? The nurse responded that she is a Christian. Norah had no idea Christians could be so kind. When Norah went home, she wanted to read more about Christianity. She read the Bible and immediately wanted a Bible for herself. She was afraid she might get in trouble if caught with one. She asked her mother's Filipino nurse if she would be able to get her an Arabic Bible. The Nurse said that she could not because she might get fired. Norah had no idea where to find a precious Bible. She knew that there was a hospital in town that had many Western doctors and nurses. She went to that hospital looking for a white person who might be a Christian that she could ask for a Bible. Ultimately, she was too afraid to do such a thing in public. So, she diligently read the Bible online. She learned everything she could about Jesus and God's word. Eventually, she came to realize that salvation and grace only come from faith in Jesus and His sacrificial blood on the cross for atonement of sin. She surrendered her life to Jesus and repented of her sin.

One day several years after the episode with the Nurse at the hospital, Norah came home to her brother snooping on her laptop. He had found that she had been reading the Bible! He confronted her and demanded to know if she had become a Christian! She asked what crime she had committed by reading the Bible. He then began to shout and hit her. Trapped and with nowhere to run, he grabbed her and began to strangle her with the apparent intent to kill her. Upon hearing the commotion, their mother ran into the room and demanded he let Norah go. She had narrowly escaped death and must be more careful, but she did not stop reading the Bible. Her family now perplexed with what to do with her as all of this cast a dark shadow over their family. It is a massive shame to have someone in the family leave Islam so they decided to marry her off to a very religious man. With little choice in the matter, our friend married the man her family set her up with.

Many years pass by. Norah has children and she has managed to keep her husband ignorant of her faith in Jesus. She was sure he would try to kill her if he knew; however, her children were getting older, and Norah wanted her children to know Jesus. She began to teach them the stories of the Bible when her husband was gone. Of course, the kids cannot always keep secrets and eventually the truth came out. He tried to reason with her to come back to Islam. She would not. He tried to beat her into submission. She would not. By this time, the whole family knew on both her side and his side that she loved Jesus. One of the men in Norah's extended family was a secret believer due to her testimony. He decided to intervene. He told Norah, "just lay low. I am trying to calm everyone down. They will let it go." To a certain degree, he was right. He was successful in getting everyone off her case for several years. At family gatherings, she began to not do the Islamic rituals during certain holidays, and again the zealous fury was unfurled anew. Several family members threw her into a full bathtub and tossed an electrical device into the water with the intent to kill her and make it look like an accident. Somehow she survived this 2nd attempted murder! Norah's male relative knew she had gone too far for him to de-escalate the situation. He felt like he had to do something drastic or else she would certainly be killed. The next day, he came to Norah and said, last night, I had a dream for how to get you out of this situation. He wanted to get her out of the country to a safer place where she would not have to be in danger any longer. He put his own life in danger so that her life could be preserved.

I cannot tell you the whole story because Norah's family would still like to track her down and kill her. I cannot tell you where she went because ultimatley, we do not know what city she ended up in. We do not wish to know. I will tell you that when we found out where she was going initially, she was in grave danger. It would not be difficult for word to get around that she was in this new country. Her culture is very tight knit and she would have been identified and picked up very quickly once word from her family got around that she had escaped. We knew she was in danger. We reached out to a couple of contacts to see if there was anyone in the country she was escaping to who would be willing to harbor Norah. All the Christians in Norah's new country knew the danger of taking her in. Everyone seemed to be afraid to help. Then, I heard that there was a family who volunteered to help. I thought I recognized the name at first but could not remember where I knew it from. All of the sudden it hit me when I read my personal email, I did know these people. I got two emails. One from a mutual friend trying to find someone willing to help Norah and one from the family who would help to rescue her. My eyes began to fill with tears because I could see God working in the situation and I knew Norah was going to be fine. Norah was terrified and traumatized when she arrived at the airport in her new country. When she found out in the car on the way to her new home that she was among friends, she was able to relax. It was comforting for her to know that her friend's (my wife) husband was friends with this family back in college, she felt relieved that she was with safe people. Ultimately, we do not know what city she lives in but we have heard that she is safe and doing well. For her safety, we do not have any contact with her.

The truth is, it took courage to harbor and help Norah. We did not have a city of refuge in the country that she was fleeing to. My friend from many years ago heard that Norah was in trouble and stepped up and became a home of refuge for Norah. Most of the people in this place did not want to help because of the potential for danger. This family who bravely stepped up are a good example of the stewards parable. They were not afraid to take a risk on behalf of their Master.

In hindsight, it is clear to me that God orchestrated all of this. When there are serious problems like there was in Norah's story, we can trust that God is orchestrating things behind the scenes. He has a way of bringing all the pieces together in a way that brings him glory. For every story that has a happy end like Norah's, we have two stories where things did not go well. Purposefully placed cities of refuge could have made the difference in those situations. The problem is, they do not exist. There are few who would be brave enough to step up and try.

Jesus said we would endure persecution before the end of the world. While we may not be experiencing suffering in our immediate circles, even now, it is happening to Jesus followers around the world. Through our journey, we have experienced the real need for cities of refuge. We are completely exhausted from seeing friends murdered, abused, and butchered. They need a safe place to run, a safe place to figure out what's next. We need centers of life preservation in every strategic place on earth yesterday!

Now, we will discuss why we have always had a need for cities of refuge. The simple answer is sin. The world is not perfect. It is unfair, unjust, and corrupt. The world has "the haves" and a lot of "have-nots." We will until the end of time need places of justice and mercy. As time get more and more difficult, this truth is more evident. In the end, four groups of people will exist.

Group 1: Is Prepared and in Bunkers Hiding
This group could be anyone inside or outside the church. They see the signs of the times and have become self-sustainable. They hope to ride out anything that may come regardless of how hard the times may become. They have planned. They have stockpiled. They have prepared. They are not interested in exposing themselves to anyone who might try to hurt them or steal their stuff. So they hide and are safe. Their hope is built on themselves, their plans, their stash, their EMF-proof basement. Their plan may even be fairly good for surviving the first portion of the apocalypse, but once Jesus arrives, judgement day will not be fun. They are goats.

Group 2: Is Prepared and Sharing
This group understands that the times are increasingly getting more concerning. They are making practical plans so that they are able to grow as much food as they can and build as many accommodations as are feasible to meet the potential needs of their community in a worst case scenario. They are bravely putting themselves out there by not hiding in a secret safe house. They have planned and stashed as well, but with the intention of sharing it and saving as many in need

as they can. Their hope and survival rests on Jesus. They are sheep.

Group 3: Is Destitute
This group could be inside or outside the church. They did or did not see that times were getting harder and did not have the ability or foresight to plan. They are naked, hungry or homeless. They are desperate. They will likely be sheep who refuse to take the mark of the beast.

Group 4: Takes the Mark of the Beast
Here, these people have no need for a city of refuge. They have the digital government currency and have taken the mark of the beast in their forehead or wrist.

Now, I want to share with you the catalyzing event that made me start to realize that there is a need for cities of refuge. Over the last 10 years, I have been an international consultant. When the COVID-19 outbreak happened, many things changed overnight. The government of the country that we were in was requiring everyone to have the the vaccine IN ORDER TO GET INTO THE GROCERY STORE. Whether you are pro-vaccine or anti vaccine is not really the point of this story. The reason for my concern is in one quick turn of events, if I did not comply to something- I could no longer buy GROCERIES. This was a massive wake up call for me. All of the sudden, I realized this sounds very similar to Revelation where those who take the mark of the beast are the only people who could buy or sell. It made me think about what are people going to do when faced with the choice of taking this mark in the forehead or wrist? How will we live or be able to work? The truth is, those of us who are not prepared will be in Group 3! We will be destitute! Group 3 will be relying on a big enough Group 2 who will take us in and give us a place to live. This was really the moment for me to realize we need to be prepared! Shortly after this epiphany, I read Matthew 24-25 and was in shock as to what I had read. It all started to make sense to me. At a minimum, we are supposed to care for the poor but those who are in the community and fellowship of Christ are a requirement for us to help. How will the world know us? It is by how we love one another. This is not a suggestion. This is an absolute requirement. When looking at the first century church, what were they doing? They were selling assets and land to make sure all the needs within the community were taken care of. There was an Ethos of radical generosity. Sacrificial hospitality was the norm. We may have to come out from among the world and live in cities of refuge and be separated. We may come to a day where we have to choose to take a mark in our forehead and wrist or refuse and suffer the consequences. Where will people go? Where will YOU go? What will YOU DO? Do we have the infrastructure in place to accommodate all of these refugees? Are we preparing now to be sustainable on our own?

What Could a City of Refuge Look Like?

For our purposes, we will get inspiration for a modern iteration of a Mosaic Levite city of refuge, from the monasteries and missions of the past and attempt to look into the future to define what is and will be needed. We can use the old terms interchangeably but ultimately, these refuge places will be our own thing. They will be what we make them! Let's make them centers of life, healing, and exponential multiplication. They are intersections where like minded people will meet and network. These cities will breathe into the weak and vulnerable and breathe out people who are strong and empowered. The DNA will be to leverage growth and sustainability for the purpose of lavish generosity. The inspiration for the structure and organization of these cities comes from a mixture of ideas from Moses and Noah on how to survive difficult times. I believe this is not really a truly new idea but a rediscovering of old ways. This is a repackaging or contextualization of the concept of monasteries which monks set up across Europe hundreds and thousands of years ago. I believe God is stirring up this movement even now! People independent of each other are beginning to think in this direction. Some are seeing the instability of the future and preparing to be self-sustainable. Others are hungry for a kingdom based community. Regardless of the reason, the reality is this is something that is happening and I am trying to understand what it is and communicate how it could impact the nations. In the past, it has been the missionaries and vocational ministers who we have sent out into the earth for penetrating the darkness. Although this had an effect, planting cities of refuge will allow the giftings, skills and talents of all to be utilized. These places will be the beach heads which will allow the good works of all the saints to be deployed in communities all over the earth as needs or opportunities arise. It is a mobilization of the many rather than the few.

Epic Hospitality

Why is hospitality so important?

It is a major undercurrent of the Bible! It may be the ultimate theme of God's relationship with man. There is much to say on this subject. It is very important. Think about it, God made a world with all sorts of good things in it and then he made us and invited us to be not only a part of this accommodation but to rule it. Of course, we messed it up by doing the one thing he asked us not to do. We were bad guests in the world he made for us. The rest of human history is a story where God has been showing us how to be a sacrificial host for ungrateful guests. He has been rolling out the red carpet stained with the blood of his son. He is preparing a new home for us to live in. He is preparing a great dinner we call the marriage supper of the lamb which I look forward to partaking in one day with you!

My wife is the one who has helped me to understand the how serious God takes hospitality. I believe that ALL people deserve lavish hospitality for one very simple reason. Humans are made in the image of God. We should honor people because God loves people. That does not mean it will be easy. Some people are very hard to love. Jesus said that you get no reward for loving people who are easy to love. I believe that there are some basic human rights. People should have access to clean water, healthy food and adequate shelter. With that said, I do believe that man should not eat if he is not willing to work but his children should not have to suffer because they have an idiot father. There is a way to make it work. Homelessness is a bad reflection on the church. Nakedness and hunger is a blight on the image of Christ followers and therefor a tarnish of our savior name. The sheep of

Jesus are actively seeking solutions to remedy these issues.

All cities of refuge should include lavish hospitality. How that plays out, this can be as diverse as the personalities, talents and giftings of the individuals involved. They don't all need to look the same, but the common denominator is hospitality.

Additional Ideas

Ultimately, the primary limitation to what a city of refuge could look like and what sorts of projects it contains is only limited by your imagination and creativity. I do not want to be too narrow about what you could do but do want to seed some ideas that could spark inspiration.

Potential Activities of a City of Refuge:

-Grow food forest
-Raise livestock
-Grow typical gardens
-Preserve food (canning or drying)
-Have daily worship gathering
-Have mobile food truck to give away meals
-Offer housing to homeless
-Housing is Airbnb rentals for income
-Have ESL classes
-Have a Training center
-Launch business incubator

-Have a community library
-Have local goods store
-Open a restaurant dining is free/donation
-Have a medical clinic
-Have a office building for entrepreneurs
-Have an art gallery
-Have an event center
-Invite the homeless into the community
-Help the jobless become self sustainable
-Feed the hungry
-Clothe the naked
-Take care of the widows
-Make room for the orphans
-Provide mental health care
-Strengthen the weak
-Be a beacon of light
-Start a 24 hour house of prayer
-Provide internship program
-Organize a community choir
-Raise a drama program
-Integrate with relief organizations
-Have herbal tea production
-Be an open heart toward the desperate

The list could go on. Take your interests and do whatever God made you passionate about. Then take that passion and use it to make the world a better and brighter place.

I hope that list caused you to get some inspiration! Each city of refuge does not need to look exactly the same with the exception of hospitality. All of those things in the list do not need to be incorporated by any means. The key here is that every community has different needs and interests. Our cities of refuge seek to tap into the local interest and try to meet any real needs that may exist. The heart of our modern monasteries is to be a hub for life giving creativity where God can show off. We want to be known for how we demonstrate God's love in real and tangible ways. We are a people who are conduits of God's unfettered goodness flowing into each other and ultimately around the world. In my opinion, there should be an easy to identify welcome center for visitors where unhinged hospitality is offered. Each person who walks into the welcome center is greeted as though he/she were Jesus Himself coming for a visit. People are treated with the upmost dignity because they are humans made in God's image. Everyone is valuable. Skin color does not matter. Ethnicity does not matter. Cultural background does not matter. Gender doesn't matter. We treat everyone with respect and dignity.

Sit down with the people you are collaborating with and think through how God would have you represent his love into your community. Think about the spoken and perhaps unspoken needs. This could happen yearly quarterly or however often you decide to get together and reevaluate your situation. All you can do is your best!

Personally, I love the idea that we could grow so much food that we can give it away in a soup kitchen either on the main monastery sites or as stand alone restaurants or mobile food trucks in the local cities and towns. The food would be so tasty that everyone would want to come in to eat! Food can be a natural gateway to network and invite the community into what we are doing. Everyone needs to eat! I know that might sounds a bit crazy to many of you. Think about it for a minute. If the food is so good that everyone would want to come eat, those who have means will want to leave a donation in the box at the back. Those who cannot; should not leave any money. People want to be a part of something that is really making a difference in the community. Whether you do this or something else, we need to think about how to get the local community involved.

Another idea I like is attracting entrepreneurs to set up business incubators in or around the monasteries. This could be the modern equivalent of the Spanish missions starting textile workshops. Office space or workshop areas could be made available to kingdom minded business people. The businesses can be natural places for the jobless in the area to find work. Once the businesses get established, they can pay rent to the monastery. Having a mature Joseph figure in leadership will help to keep the vision focused. There is always a temptation to serve mammon. We produce abundance so that we can provide for our families but in the end, it all belongs to

God. As we have been freely given to, we must freely give. We never serve money. Money serves the needs of the community. You cannot take it with you when you die! You might as well put it to good use while you are alive.

I will only add one more thing. Whatever talents you have been given by the Master is what you will be judged on, how you deployed them. Use what you have. Do the best you can with what you have. Do not worry about what you cannot do. If you are faithful with what you have, the master said he will give you more later. Our goal is to wisely invest the resources that God has entrusted us with.

Where do I start?

Seek out other likeminded people. Come find us or others who are working to build cities of refuge.

Do what you can with what you have. This is what I am really hoping will happen. I would love to see millions of you out there start cities of refuge in every corner of earth. Here are some ideas and resources that we have learned and gathered along our journey that will hopefully help you in yours. I do not want to be prescriptive here of what you should do but rather be descriptive of what others have done that might inspire you or shape your thoughts.

-Use what you have. Take an inventory how much land, skills and/or resources you have available to you.
-Once you have a good inventory, think about what you would like to do. Not every city of refuge has to operate and focus on the same things. For example, one's land might not be close to an urban population with tons of homeless people but might be great for growing huge amounts of food. What you can focus on trying to accomplish could be within the skill sets of who you have with you and what resources you have available to you.
-If you are in a rural area where needs are limited, you can network with groups who are working in high need areas. You can donate your excesses to support those with big needs.

Make two lists.
Point A: Current position.
Point B: Where you would like to be.
Goal setting: Break down in actionable steps how you can get from Point A to Point B.

One with your desires and the other with what you have. Then focus on the things that align. Pray for people to come along who can help implement the things you would like to do but are lacking in skills or resources to do.

Here is an example that will illustrate what I am talking about. Your list should be unique to your skills, interests and resources that are available to you.

What We Have:
-Have 3 tiny homes + 40 acres
-Have 5 acres of free land
-Have 25 acres of pasture land
-Skilled in raising sheep
-Skilled in permaculture
-Skilled in building structures

What We Would Like to do:

-House refugees
-Grow permaculture food forest
-Have a training centre
-Invite other likeminded families to join
-Need ESL teachers or educators
-Raising Sheep
-Able to feed a community of 5,000

-Expand growing capacity of food

I think it is good to raise the bar high to want to do more than you can. I would recommend that you do what you can and ask God to provide so that you can do more. Be faithful with what you have! Your list dose not need to look exactly like the one above. There are many great things you could do to be a blessings to your community and the world. I would encourage you to focus on what you are passionate about.

Now that you are focused on what you would like to do and what is a reasonable target, let us think about what would be a good practical place to start. Many people can get themselves tripped up here by trying to do too much at once. Take your list of what you want and merge it with your list of what you have and lets organize it based on priority.

ACTIONABLE STEPS:
-Plant a 4 acre food forest and 1 acre monoculture (yearly veggies) = production of 40,000-50,000 pounds of food. This can fully feed 20-25 people per year

-Purchase 10 sheep to start growing flock

-Use 3 tiny homes as temporary housing for new families as they build a permanent residence.

-Once 3 new families are settled with their own home perhaps start thinking about taking in homeless. Where do we put them? Maybe we can start reducing the pasture land to allow for refugee housing? Perhaps we can buy more land? Perhaps a new family wanting to collaborate will have land to settle these new refugees?

-Build training centre and put the word out of teachers to come. 1st teacher can stay in a tiny home.

-Pray about expanding the co-op to add enough growers to see food production capacity meet all the potential need for food of the 5,000 people in the county.

-In the above example, we focus on growing food first. This will generate potential income to do more. It allows for the opportunity to give food away to those in need. The big thing is that it increases sustainability for expansion.

-The purchase of sheep is 2nd only because more food can be produced through permaculture. Once the food forest is planted, there is minimal maintenance needed and the focus can shift to maintaining and caring for the daily needs of the flock. If you have enough people to start with, doing both the food forest and the flock could happen at the same time.

-The tiny homes could be utilized at anytime to facilitate new comers who want to join. You could take in homeless here. If that is what you feel God leading to do, then by all means go for it! It might be easier to take in a missionary family coming back from the field or a family in the church who lost their job and/or home. They could be old friends from college or high school who love what you are doing and want to jump in. God will bring the right people in the right time. If you did decided to carve up the pasture land for people to settle on, you can build some apartment complex or a do allotments of half acre plots with a home and food forest surrounding it. This would increase your housing capacity as well as your food productivity. What you are sacrificing is your protein source in the lamb meat. In order to build homes you need a builder! Pray the Lord will bring a builder.

-This might be a time to think about acquiring more land. If you are able to sell off the excess food from the sheep farm and permaculture production, you could have more money. Of course, if the needs in the community are great, you may have given away quite a bit of food. At any rate, hopefully you can think about purchasing more land. Maybe someone in the community sees what you are doing and might donate land? Pray the Lord will provide so that you can expand....if you want to expand. Having that extra land will allow you to not have to sacrifice your sheep pasture and provide areas for expansion of homesteads or additional food production.

-Now that you have a thriving community, perhaps now is the time to take on something a bit more ambitious. Let's build a school for the children or maybe an ESL centre for the foreign refugees you have taken or plan to take in.

-Now that you have a movement, it might be time to organize a city of refuge co-op. I pray that the Lord will raise up other families and communities around you who are doing the similar things. I think you will know the right time to do this because the need to co-operate and help each other will grow. One family may have a real passion for hospitality and take in too many refugees. Another family may be very good at raising livestock but not really involved with much else. On your city of refuge, you may have phased out your sheep pasture and now need meat and protein. You can trade with each other or give as the Lord leads. The key is to pray often together and regularly discuss the needs of the community with the heart to meet any needs that arise as best as possible. This will allow for future planning of what needs to be grown or how many houses need to be built based on changing needs and situation. Clear communication is essential.

You do not need to do what I just outlined. This is only an example of how you could start thinking through what you want to do and how to prioritize. God made you in a unique way with a certain skill set. Take that skill set and do what you can do. There is no shame in focusing only on one thing if that is the thing God made you to do. It will bless the others in your county or region if you are excelling at what God made you to do. Not everyone needs to "live" at the city of refuge. Being in close proximity is enough. Collaboration is the way forward!

Can My Church be involved?

YES! There are many ways a church can be involved with developing cities of refuge. A church could facilitate being a refuge and/or supporting it's members who are starting one or supporting one in the community.

Practical ways churches can collaborate with cities of refuge:
-Identify a Joseph or many Josephs and stand behind them in support.
-A church can take on the mantle of being a hub for being a city of refuge in a community which can take on many forms.
-Many churches have excess land that is not being utilized and can be developed to grow a garden, food forest, housing capacity and/or a site for a soup kitchen.
-Organize volunteers to work with a local city of refuge.
-Financially support a city of refuges.
-Many different partnerships can develop. A church may have an addictions program that cities of refuge can send people to. A church may have a counseling ministry that can be of support of people coming through cities of refuge.

How can a City of Hospitality be Sustainable?

The goal is to produce more goods than the charitable needs of the community. This may sound easier said than done in some places where poverty and the needs are great. That is the reason we need to band together. Communities that have little to no need can give and volunteer in places that have extensive need. We should strive for sustainability at a minimum with the desire to produce an excess which can be traded or sold for a profit. There is a risk that goats get into positions of authority and make bad decisions. There is potential for groups or locations to lose sight of the mission and turn the monastery into a casino. My advice is to support leaders who have the heart of Joseph. Avoid leaders who seem to say the right things but only focus on money or profit margins. Look at what the leaders do and focus less on what they say. Actions speak louder than words and illuminate the true intentions of a person's heart. The goal of a city of refuge is to be a haven of hospitality and safety net for the community in the event of a serious crisis. Leadership should be there to help solve or remedy as best it can the troubles of the community that it serves. The generation of products or goods are with the idea that if there is a need, we can give liberally to meet the needs. If there are no needs, then the products or goods can be sold into the market and those monies or resources can be invested locally or abroad as the Lord may lead your group. Just do not bury the money. Use it! Trust the Lord to give you more later if you need more. Of course leave a reserve that is reasonable for a rainy day. It may be wise to leave a cushion of savings for unexpected challenges that could arise.

Words of Caution

We are learning just like you on how to do this better. I hope we can update this portion of the book in the future as we learn more of the potential points of conflict and pitfalls. For now, here are some of the words of caution to look out for and strategies we think could help avoid trouble. Of course we could be wrong and if you think we are please do what you believe God is calling you to do. This section only serves to tell you where we have seen painful situations and difficulties and where it could perhaps be avoided.

-Family partnerships seems to create dynamics for big conflict. Especially if land is purchased together. We have seen people lose land and get into major power struggles over what will be done with the land. I personally believe this can be eliminated by having the land owned by one person and anyone who comes to live either buys a plot or a plot is given to them to administer however they want. It might be wise to make monasteries a 501c3 non-profit. Smaller operations can be owned by individuals but I would recommend that large operations be administered as non-profit organizations.

-<u>Who should lead?</u> One of the principles that we see is that the cities of refuge, monasteries, and missions where administered by the priests. I personally believe that the leaders should be the ones most like Joseph. People who are just and compassionate. These people should have some administrative dimension in their skill set.

-<u>Every man has his own land</u>: I have taken this principle from Micah 4:4. Every man will sit under his Vine and fig tree. No one will be able to make him afraid. If every family has their own land that is fruitful, then they will have no need to be fearful of how they will sustain themselves or who might come to try to take advantage of them. I would encourage you to make sure that when vulnerable people come to you, that they are positioned to be self sustainable and empowered. Otherwise, unscrupulous people will take advantage of them. The goal should be to elevate people not to subjugate people. It would be horrendous to take in the refugee only to enslave them. Freely have you been given to and freely you should give.

-<u>Own the land outright</u>: It should not have to be said, but do NOT try to start a COR on someone else's land. It is not wise. You are not positioning yourself or the people you take in to be prepared. The owner can pull the land out from under you, raise rent exorbitantly after you have invested in building it up. I have seen people go in together and try to get a loan or owner finance a piece of property. They lost the land because ONE did not make payments and then all of the thousands of man hours and dollars were lost. Everyone's investments were lost because of mismanagement of a few people. If the land is held in a 501c3, it might be even better. I would recommend that you do not invite people to invest in your land and build houses and plant food forest if you do not own it out right. If you lose it, they can too. Cities of refuge should be placed on land that is fully owned. This is my opinion based on experience.

-Don't be a cult: If you believe some weird things, do not spread your weird ideas around. I know that sounds harsh. We all have disagreements over things in scripture on some level. Even my wife and I do not agree on every single thing. Do not allow someone given to weird ideas to get into authority positions. False teaching should be identified and challenged quickly. The scriptures are the authority and strange doctrines should be marginalized. I do know the term strange doctrine might mean different things to different people. The point is to hold each other accountable to what the word of God says. Be like the Berean people.

How We Can Help

What sort of group are you in? Sheep or goat? The main thing is whether people are sheep. THEN the idea that they are living the sheep way. Let's keep the main thing THE MAIN THING. Now, if you are a sheep- what kind of things are you doing to indicate you are a sheep? What could be done differently?

I am asking you as an individual, what are you doing? Who do you hang out with? What term would you say best describes the ETHOS of your group? These are personal questions for you to think about. Which group would you personally fall into? I do not think it is too late...yet. That is why I am writing this book.

Let us bravely enter the end of this age with our torches held high and with oil burning bright. I am calling on all groups to make preparations just as Joseph did to meet the unimaginable need and suffering people are experiencing. I personally believe that one very effective strategy for the sheep of Jesus is to set up cities of refuge! We can pool resources and set up these centers of hospitality and agriculture where we can house the strangers and feed the hungry. These bastions of hope should not be money sink holes but should be sustainable resource generators. These are incubators where jobs and products are created just as Basil did in Caesarea and the Spanish missionaries did at the Alamo.

If you do not see any groups around you loving like Jesus did, then you have a couple of options:

Fill your torches with oil and shine locally. Make your homestead a center of giving and hospitality. Others will join you who share this Ethos. You can prepare as best as you can to be the Joseph in your community. Find the others in your area who feel the same as you do. Work together! Spend time regularly together so you can know who has needs.

Another option is to move to be near a community that shares the Ethos of Basil. If you do not feel like you are able to be a catalyst in your community, perhaps you can support a city of refuge in another place.

Regardless of which direction you decide to go. I want to invite you to be a part of a global movement. God is raising up leaders in every corner of the Earth to be his sheep and shine brightly in this coming dark time. We will have a non-profit where funds and real-estate can be donated and support the establishment of cities of refuge all over the earth. We desire to see sustainable cities of hospitality planted in every strategic forgotten crossroads of the earth. We want you to do your thing in your community and shine brightly there. There is a need for resources to be deployed in areas that are underserved or do not have the ability to start up themselves because of poverty or other issues.

Some of the needs are:
-Short term volunteers to build structures and plant food forest
-Long term settlers to help establish new or struggling cities of refuge
-Real-estate to be able to set up more cities of refuge
-$$$ to invest in sustainable cities of refuge
-Share about this book and movement on social media

There are many positions that could be used in cities of refuge as they emerge. This list is not exhaustive. I am sure there is a need for the unique skills that you have.

Practical Needs:
-Architects

-Artists
-Canners and Food Preservers
-Engineers
-Teachers
-Entrepreneurs
-Arborists
-Trauma Counselors
-Pastors
-Permaculture Experts
-Finance Experts
-Event Planners
-Farmers
-Animal Husbandry
-Nurses
-Builders
-Doctors
-Cooks/Chefs
-Musicians
-Hospitality Managers
-House Keeping
-Electricians
-Plumbers
-Funders or Givers
-Mothers
-Fathers

MANY MORE needs!
We are working to create places where people who want to be involved can collaborate and pool resources to where they are needed. All inquires, questions or comments, please send to: refugecities@gmail.com

[1] H.E.L.P.S Ministries Inc. . (2021). 1482. Ethnikos. Strong's Greek: 1482. ἐθνικός (ethnikos) -- national, foreign, i.e. Spec. A Gentile. https://biblehub.com/greek/1482.htm

www.ingramcontent.com/pod-product-compliance
Lightning Source LLC
Chambersburg PA
CBHW072336270726
48659CB00022B/1714